THE HIGHLANDERS

Okiufa man, Asaro, in dancing costume. He carries a blackpalm bow and a
bundle of arrows. Cassowary plumes form the basis of his headdress. Parrot
feathers, white cuscus skin, *tambu* shell and scarab beetles provide most
of the facial decoration

JAMES SINCLAIR

THE HIGHLANDERS

The Jacaranda Press with Robert Brown and Associates

First published 1971 by
JACARANDA PRESS PTY LTD
46 Douglas Street, Milton, Q.
32 Church Street, Ryde, N.S.W.
37 Little Bourke Street, Melbourne, Vic.
142 Colin Street, West Perth, W.A.
298a Grange Road, Flinders Park, S.A.
57 France Street, Auckland, N.Z.
P.O. Box 3395, Port Moresby, P.N.G.

Typesetting by Queensland Type Service, Brisbane
Printed in Hong Kong

© James Sinclair 1971

National Library of Australia
Card Number and ISBN 0 7016 0510 3

BY THE SAME AUTHOR

Behind the Ranges, Melbourne University Press, 1966
The Outside Man, Lansdowne Press, Melbourne, 1969
Sepik Pilot, Lansdowne Press, Melbourne, 1971

IN PREPARATION

Wigmen of Papua, Jacaranda Press, Brisbane

Back jacket
Pretty Yagaria girls, Lufa Sub-District. Their home is in the shadow of Mount Michael. Necklets are made from trade beads, imported from Italy and Germany

Front jacket
Nodofonoyufa man in ceremonial dress. These people have an intense love of highly colourful decoration

Endpapers
Copper panel made by Eddy Scotti, a student from the Art Department, Goroka Teachers College. This beautiful work features a traditional design

Title page
A little hamlet in the North Fore, Okapa Sub-District, photographed just after dawn

Designed by Barbara Hutley

To James Lindsay Taylor

James Lindsay Taylor with the author *(left)*

Author's Note

This is primarily a book of photographs: inevitably, in a book of this type, the text is too brief to do justice to the subject. Many books have been written on the Highlands, and there is a large and growing volume of anthropological writings on every conceivable aspect of the daily life of the Highlanders. Much of this material is available in specialized books, but perhaps more may be found scattered through the pages of learned journals not normally available to the general reader. For the use of those who would like to read more deeply on the Highlanders a brief reading list is given below. This covers only books currently in print, and likely to be of interest to those with a general interest only in the subject. The anthropological periodical *Oceania* is available at many large public libraries.

New Guinea: The Last Unknown. Gavin Souter. Angus and Robertson, Sydney, 1963.
Plumes and Arrows. Colin Simpson. Angus and Robertson, Sydney, 1963.
The High Valley. Kenneth E. Read. George Allen and Unwin Ltd, London, 1966.
Excess and Restraint. Ronald M. Berndt. University of Chicago Press, 1962.
Pigs, Pearlshell and Women. A Symposium edited by R. M. Glasse and M. J. Meggitt. Prentice-Hall, New Jersey, 1969.
From Stone to Steel. Richard F. Salisbury. Melbourne University Press, 1962.
Behind the Ranges. James Sinclair. Melbourne University Press, 1966.
Oceania. The University of Sydney. Quarterly publication, with many articles from time to time on the Highlanders.

In writing the text I have made reference to a wide range of published work, and also to an unpublished sub-thesis by Ian Willis of the Institute of Technology, Lae, on the 1930 journey of Leahy and Dwyer, and to a mass of detailed material collected by Captain Ian Grabowsky bearing on the history of civil aviation in Papua and New Guinea. To these gentlemen I express my thanks.

I would also like to thank the pilots of the Goroka-based charter company, Territory Air Lines, for their skill and co-operation in the making of the aerial photographs in this book.

Daulo Pass country

Contents

Introduction

This book tells principally of the people of the Eastern Highlands, one of the four Highlands districts of Papua and New Guinea and the first to be penetrated by expeditions from the long-settled coast.

Of all the districts of Papua and New Guinea, the Highlands are by Nature the most favoured. Straddling the territorial border, the superb grassed valleys, the towering mountains and the cool refreshing climate of these districts set them apart. The layman's picture of New Guinea — sweltering heat, torrential rain, jungle, swamps, fever — is true of much of the Territory, but it has no application to the Highlands. Here we find a land of high valleys — five thousand feet high — clasped and upheld by a chain of mountains that rise to eleven, thirteen, even fifteen thousand feet, blessed with a climate that is perennial spring, free from the scourge of tropical disease, with rainfall and soils capable of coaxing forth almost any kind of temperate crops. Everyday living is so different in the Highlands that one could well be in another country altogether.

The Highlanders themselves are a strong and colourful race, with many regional differences in dress, in decoration, in language and in culture. And yet these people are generally akin. They are tough-minded, conservative, physically robust, slow to change and often suspicious of the motives of the better educated people of the coast and the islands.

Between them, the four Highlands districts — Eastern, Western and Southern Highlands and the Chimbu — contain over nine hundred thousand of the estimated two and a quarter millions of the people of Papua and New Guinea. The Highlanders will without doubt exercise a powerful influence on the future development of this country. For they share so many common traits and characteristics that the hundreds of disparate linguistic and cultural groups who inhabit the other fourteen districts of this Territory look upon the Highlanders as, indeed, one people.

Labogai mother and child (Lufa)

A Yagaria man, from near Mount Michael. Note the blackpalm bow, strengthened with cane lashings and strung with bamboo. The broad-bladed arrow is of bamboo, and designed to kill pigs

Watabung man glares fiercely at the camera. His pig tusks are particularly fine

Above: Gawoi boy

Left: Little Frigano girl in ceremonial dress

Far left: Woman of the Gahuku, Asaro Valley. She is dressed for dancing

One of the famous 'mudmen' of the Asaro

Pretty young girl from the Frigano in ceremonial dress

Little Daulo boy with wildflowers

Asaro man — a leader of his clan

Page xviii: Marawaka belle. Her beads come from the trade store

Page xix: Unggai woman. Her face is painted in characteristic patterns with coloured clays dug from the earth

xvii

I

Discovery

It is our conceit that the history of lands previously unknown begins only with exploration by our own kind. We tend to ignore existing cultures and institutions, for they are different from our own and thus, inevitably, must be inferior. Many peoples with ancient cultures have been looked upon as crude barbarians by invading vanguards of Western races, and by and large the English speaking peoples have been the most complacent, the most blind.

When the first explorers began to touch upon the forbidding coastline of unknown New Guinea, they were invariably repelled by the native peoples they encountered, and perhaps understandably, for although the Melanesians had lived in this island for thousands of years, they had failed to develop any accepted civilization in the Western sense. They had no common language, religion, or recorded history. They were fierce tribesmen, split into hundreds of mutually hostile, isolated groups, spending their sum of days in killing, hating, distrusting each other. In the Western sense, they had no architecture, no literature, no legal system, no technology. A man would live and die unenlightened, within the tight confines of his tribal group, afraid to venture far; every day of his usually short life he spent in mortal fear: fear of his enemies, of magic, of the unknown.

The anthropologists have shown us that the traditional New Guinea society was in no way contemptible, even if utterly different from our own. It was a society shaped and conditioned by the harsh, broken geography of the island. As the years progressed and the blank spaces on the maps were slowly and painfully filled, the numbers of enumerated New Guinea tribal groups swelled into many hundreds. By the end of the second decade of the present century, it was thought that few tribes remained to be discovered. The island groups, the coastal plains and much of the interior had been explored by patrols and brought under control. The day of the aeroplane had not yet come and the great mountains that barred the way into the interior of the mainland were thought to extend indefinitely, unpopulated except perhaps for roaming bands of nomads and cannibals. The aeroplane would very quickly have demonstrated the error of this assumption, but the first flight would not be made in the Highlands until November 1929. And so, as the fourth decade of

A fine village leader from the Yagaria. There is force and character in every line of his face

our century commenced, one huge empty space remained in the centre of the map of New Guinea, covering an area of 24,000 square miles.

*　　　*　　　*

The emergence of the Highlanders from their centuries of mountain-girt isolation really began in 1928, when a quiet prospector, Ned Rowlands, walked with a handful of carriers to the head of the Markham River and across the Bismarck Ranges to the Ramu headwaters, looking for gold. He found it, on the Ornapinka River. Gold lured Rowlands on, further than any white man had hitherto gone, and it was the lure of gold that finally unlocked the secrets of the Highlands.

The fringes of the Highlands had been touched upon years before. Leonhardt Flierl, the Lutheran missionary, had visited Puntibasa, on the extreme eastern edge of what is today the Gadsup Census Division of the Kainantu Sub-District, as far back as 1922. Four years later Flierl established a sub-station of his Mission at Lihona, a village on the northern fall of the Bismarcks. Flierl crossed the mountains from Lihona, and it has been claimed that he penetrated as far as Bena Bena, but this is doubtful. In 1923 the Australian forester, Lane-Poole, climbed Mt Otto and almost became the first European to see the valleys of the Eastern Highlands. In 1924, J. Appelby, an Assistant District Officer of the Administration, visited the Puntibasa-Binamarien area. In 1928 tribal fighting broke out between the Puntibasa and Binamarien people; the Binamarien were driven down to the Markham Valley. They appealed to the Administration for help, and a patrol came up the Markham and re-established the Binamarien on their tribal lands. Two further Administration patrols were made to the Arau people, some distance to the south, to settle inter-tribal fighting. In 1926 and again in 1929 the District Officer, Madang, Captain Hunter, made initial patrols into the Upper Ramu Valley; another Madang patrol even made an initial census of villages above the 5,000-foot level who had never before seen a white man. The first Mission station in what is today the Eastern Highlands was established in 1931 by the Rev. W. Bergmann of the Lutheran Mission at Kambaidam.

Ned Rowlands' journeys took him west of Kainantu, and although his wanderings have little historical importance of themselves, they were to have momentous consequences, for a confidential report on his discovery was sufficient to interest the pioneer Morobe Goldfields company, Guinea Gold No Liability, in the Upper Ramu. The company asked C. J. Levien, ex-Administration District Officer and the true father of Bulolo Gold Dredging Limited, to go in and find Ned Rowlands and test his discovery for possible large scale development.

Levien was in Sydney where he had semi-permanently settled, but in mid-February 1929 he sailed for New Guinea on the Burns Philp vessel *Montoro*; by early April he was walking up the broad Markham Valley with six carriers to Sangan, a village on the valley floor some seventy miles from the coast, and here he constructed a tiny aerodrome, the first to be built anywhere in New Guinea away from the

Chimbu country

Duna (Southern Highlands) man

Huri (Southern Highlands) fight-leader

Morobe Goldfields. Levien, far-sighted, the first man to realize the vital part that aeroplanes could play in the development of the Goldfields, was determined to use the aeroplane to assist him in his present task. The strip completed, he walked back to Lae and on 25 May flew in to Sangan in a Guinea Airways Junkers W34. In fourteen days a total of fifteen landings were made at Sangan as Levien built up his supplies for the walk over the mountains to find Rowlands. Months of walking and thousands of hours of human effort were saved by flying supplies from the coast to Sangan. The 'leap-frog' technique thus pioneered by Levien was to be used in the coming years to open the Highlands.

The Sangan base established, Levien crossed the mountains and entered the Arona Valley. 'A most wonderful vista,' he later reported. 'What had been thought to be heavy mountains turned out to be magnificent rolling downs covered with grass and practically no timber, and one could look over 20 to 25 miles of country from one point.'

Moving west, Levien encountered large bands of stalwart, armed men; at one stage his carriers were on the verge of running, but he kept on and found Rowlands. He stayed long enough to convince himself that Rowlands' discovery was worth further investigation, then walked back to Lae, leaving his surplus stores with the prospector.

In September, two Lutheran missionaries, Dr G. Pilhofer and the Rev. W. Bergmann, left Lihona, crossed the Bismarcks and entered the Dunantina Valley. They followed this down for some distance then turned to the east, catching a glimpse of the densely-populated Bena Bena Valley, and entered the headwaters of the Ramu, west of the present station of Kainantu. On their way to the Upper Markham, they came across Rowlands' camp and learned for the first time that they had been beaten to the Ramu headwaters. No reports were issued by the Mission on this journey; it was many years before the general public was made aware of the important exploratory work carried out by the Lutheran Mission in the Huon Peninsula and the fringes of the Highlands.

In November 1929 Levien flew back to Sangan, and in a Guinea Airways Moth piloted by Frank Drayton, he made an aerial survey of the Arona-Kainantu area — the first known use of an aeroplane in New Guinea for purely exploratory purposes. The survey took one hour and forty minutes, and Levien estimated that this saved him three weeks of abortive walking, for he came back with a sound idea of the country that he planned to walk over with Ned Rowlands.

On 14 November, Levien and his little band again crossed the ranges to Rowlands' camp, and using supplies that had been carried in over preceding weeks from the Sangan base the two men and their armed carriers set off on a prospecting expedition. They undoubtedly covered a lot of new ground, and encountered many tribes for the first time, but in the absence of their maps it is not possible today to follow their route. They met with some hostility; in the Yonki country, where Rowlands had his main camp, they were forced to open fire on an arrow-firing crowd after a carrier had been wounded in the stomach.

Levien left the intrepid Rowlands and arrived back in Lae on 10 December 1929. He told his company that he did not think that the Upper Ramu was suitable for large-scale development, although doubtless offering prospects to individual miners. Shortly afterwards Placer Development — with which company Guinea Gold was associated — decided to go ahead with the daring plan to use aircraft to develop the Bulolo leases, a decision that led to the formation of Bulolo Gold Dredging Limited and the expansion of the gold industry in New Guinea on a scale hitherto undreamed-of. The Upper Ramu was forgotten.

In March 1930, Ned Rowlands walked out of the Upper Ramu and announced publicly that he had found payable gold on the Ornapinka. He emphasized that the find was a small one. But his warning went unheeded. The Morobe miners had gold fever. The fabulously rich and easy alluvial gold of Edie Creek, high in the mountains above the Wau Valley, discovered in 1926 by the prospectors, W. G. Royal and R. M. Glasson, was by now almost gone; only major operators were now making money there. Where was the source of Rowlands' gold, they asked? Surely experienced men could follow the gold and so perhaps find another Edie Creek, another chance for the individual prospector to make his fortune. They decided to finance an expedition to go and see.

The journey that resulted was quite unwittingly to unlock the front door to the Highlands, and must therefore be acknowledged as one of the supremely important journeys of modern New Guinea history.

On 6 April 1930, twenty-five miners met at Edie Creek to finalize their plans. They jointly contributed the sum of $302 to finance the venture and offered one of their number, Michael J. Leahy, the leadership of the expedition. So began the remarkable career of one of the foremost of New Guinea's explorers.

Mick Leahy had come to New Guinea like so many others in 1926, to make his fortune at Edie Creek. Like so many others, he failed, and in 1930 was working with his brother, Jim, on the Wau-Edie Creek road, a section of which they held on contract. Working with them was Michael Dwyer. Leahy and Dwyer were bush-wise, experienced prospectors and in hard physical condition. Both were convinced that another Edie Creek must be somewhere in the mountains, waiting to be found. They accepted the offer to make the expedition.

Leahy and Dwyer had no intention of conducting a major exploratory expedition. They were hard-headed prospectors and at this stage they were interested only in gold. They intended only to follow up Ned Rowlands' colours of gold to the source, and then return to report their findings to their sponsors. They wasted no time. Leahy was in Salamaua the day after the meeting, buying equipment and supplies.

After considerable delays in relaying their supplies to a base camp at Kaigulan, in the Ramu Valley, they ascended the flanks of the Bismarck Range to the Lutheran Mission station at Lihona, from where they planned to carry out trips until they picked up Rowlands' tracks. Leahy had heard rumours of the journeys of Flierl,

The Arona Valley, Kainantu

An empty hut on a high ridge near the source of the Dunantina

The beautiful Dunantina some miles down from the source — the valley is starting to open up

Pilhofer and Bergmann and expected that the river valley they had followed, the Dunantina, was also the valley in which Rowlands had found his gold. They planned to travel downstream to his claim, prospecting the tributaries as they went.

Leahy had not had the advantage of a prior aerial examination of the country that he and Dwyer would walk over to guide him, and in consequence the strange geography of the Highlands fooled him. Rowlands' find was on the watershed of the Ramu; all the streams in the grassed valleys walked over by Rowlands and Levien emptied to the north via the Ramu into the Bismarck Sea. The Dunantina, barely ten miles west of Rowlands' Ornapinka, and all of the other streams that lay, undiscovered, to the west for more than one hundred miles, emptied via the huge Purari River system into the Papuan Gulf, through the great Central Ranges to the south. As Leahy and Dwyer and their tiny band of sixteen armed carriers moved down the green valley of the beautiful Dunantina from where it began as a mere trickle of water, high in the mountains, through and beyond the Kamano groups first visited by the Lutherans, they found themselves forced always to the south, away from the Ramu and the longed-for source of Rowlands' gold.

The Kamano, a powerful and populous people, looked upon the white men as spirits, the returned ghosts of long dead ancestors — a reaction common among Highland groups upon their first encounter with the European — and they eagerly but fearfully pressed around the camps of this strange invading force as, day after day, Leahy and Dwyer prospected their way down the lush valley, past the stockaded villages and through vast fenced gardens of sweet potato, taro and bananas, eloquent proof of the gardening skill of these people of the Dunantina. They daily expected to come across the camp of Ned Rowlands; they were astounded at the extent of the populations they were encountering, in what had been thought to be the dead heart of New Guinea. Near the village of Kafetegu, close to the junction of the Dunantina with another stream, the Kamamentina, Leahy and Dwyer climbed a spur and saw, away to the west, a great grassed valley, dappled with gardens and streaked with the blue smoke of countless cooking fires: the Asaro, one of the characteristic valley systems of the Highlands and the site of the present town of Goroka. They suspected then that the Highlands populations must be immense.

They were tempted to go and explore the Asaro, but this would have taken them even further away from Ned Rowlands and his gold. They continued down the Dunantina, but the river held relentlessly to the south and as day succeeded day it was forced upon them that the river they were following could not be the Ramu.

The country was guiding them south, towards a vast, jagged mountain range that culminated in a broken, many-tiered peak, 12,300 feet high, that we know today as Mount Michael, in honour of the two Michaels who were the first white men to approach it. They left the land of the Kamano and entered upon the territory of the Yagaria, who lived in small stockaded settlements on ridges and folds of their rolling grasslands. Again the people, bewildered by these strangers and their equipment, their tents and their knives and axes of steel, thronged the camps of the prospectors.

Heavily larded with evil-smelling pig grease, as a measure against the biting cold of this high country, the people showed such insatiable curiosity, such apprehension, attraction and fear all intermixed, that Leahy and Dwyer were hard put to maintain even tempers. As they approached Mount Michael they climbed; the nights sparkled with the glint and glow of thousands of cook fires.

Still the river valley held to the south. They were now following the course of what we call today the Asaro; as they neared the mountain, the river-gorge deepened and the going became harder; then, on 11 June 1930, they came to a great river, joining their stream, flowing in from the north-west. It was the Wahgi, powerful, full-flowing, a mightier stream than the Asaro. The prospectors climbed down to the great river and over the days that followed they found swollen corpses, borne down from the unknown country to the west; bones, and sometimes human skulls, could be seen on the river terraces. Obviously, an even greater population lived in that western country.

Leahy and Dwyer now had no doubt that they had chanced upon a new river-system, and they were so deeply into the unknown that they determined to go on, following the flow of the water until it came to its destination; their stores were almost exhausted and they did not relish the thought of turning back upon their tracks. They had no real idea of where they were; clearly, the theories held about the nature of the interior were all wrong, but they knew that if they followed the river — below the Asaro-Wahgi junction it becomes the Tua — they must eventually reach the sea. So on the tiny party went.

The Tua runs through deep and rocky defiles, and the little party moved slowly through scattered populations as the Tua led them west, and then again south. They were moving through densely bushed forest, far different from the wonderful grasslands of the Dunantina and the Yagaria. Food supplies were failing. Many times they were forced away from the river, but whenever their guides led them back they saw more dead bodies, more bones in the sand, all carried down from savage battlegrounds in the great grassed western valleys by the Wahgi.

In mid-June the prospectors left the Tua and passed through the isolated populations living around the deeply eroded flanks of the lonely mountain, Karimui. Travelling was now desperately hard. Canned foods virtually finished, they traded with the Mikaru people — to whom the strangers were supermen, descended from the skies — for sago, poor food to those unaccustomed to it.

And so they travelled on, to the Pio River — which joins with the Erave flowing out of the Southern Highlands, to form the great Purari. They did not know it, but they were deep into Papua and heading away from the grasslands towards the Gulf of Papua. Many privations lay before them — flooded rivers, the fearsome Hathor Gorge, the uncertainty of the unknown — before to their astonishment they gained the Papuan coast, on 10 July 1930. They had crossed New Guinea.

Leahy and Dwyer by their extraordinary journey laid to rest, once and for all, the myth of the arid heart of New Guinea. It is for this that the journey is so important

Lufa country, where Leahy and Dwyer walked

Tua country, where Leahy and Dwyer walked. Taken just after dawn

Page 14: Lufa man

Page 15: Yagaria woman

Mount Michael at dusk

The Highlands Highway as the dawn
mists start to lift

in the history of the exploration of the interior, for although the discoveries made by Leahy and Dwyer created virtually no initial interest, their journey marked the beginning of the rapid exploration of the Highlands.

In October and November, Leahy and Dwyer went back and explored the valleys of the Bena Bena and the Asaro. This was the last work that the two prospectors carried out together in the Highlands. After this journey — they found traces of gold — they both returned to the Morobe Goldfields. In 1931 Dwyer, Leahy and his brother Pat were commissioned by the big English-financed company, New Guinea Goldfields, to make prospecting expeditions into what was then known as the Kukukuku country, and it was during the journey of the Leahy brothers into the Langimar River that they were attacked and wounded by the savage little bark-cloaked Kukukuku. But Mick Leahy did not forget the Highlands.

Ned Rowlands remained in the Ramu. He was no longer the only miner on the field; E. Ubanks, A. J. Peadon, Karkar Smith and others were working claims, and gradually others came in. Then there appeared on the scene the second giant figure in the history of the exploration of the Highlands: James Lindsay Taylor.

Jim Taylor, Assistant District Officer based at Salamaua, walked into the Upper Ramu in June 1932. The first airstrip in the Highlands, at Lapumpa, near the present site of Kainantu, had just been constructed by A. J. Peadon and Patrol Officer Alan Ross. The initial landing was made on the strip by Bob Gurney on 2 September, in a Fox Moth of Guinea Airways. Soon the Junkers F13 of Guinea Airways was flying to Lapumpa. The strip proved to be inadequate for the larger Junkers W34, and Taylor commenced to construct the present Kainantu strip. The provision of an airstrip greatly accelerated the development of the Upper Ramu. The aeroplane was established, and would prove to be essential in the swift-moving exploration of the next few years.

The next stage in the opening of the Highlands came in October 1932. Major Harrison, general manager of New Guinea Goldfields, anxious to locate new gold-bearing areas suitable for major development, again commissioned Mick Leahy to lead a prospecting party, this time back to the Bena country that he and Dwyer had examined. With his young brother Dan, Leahy took in the company's geologist, H. M. Kingsbury, and his assistant, Robert Whyte, and they briefly examined the Bena country; the company men then flew back to Wau from Lapumpa to report, leaving the Leahys to walk back to the Bena where, on 20 December, they marked out a small airstrip near Gauritufa Creek.

The construction of an airstrip in New Guinea today takes many months, even years; the Department of Civil Aviation insists upon most careful standards, for today's aeroplanes are sophisticated, highly engineered machines. The aeroplanes of 1932 were simple and robust, and no officer of D.C.A. had ever set foot in the Highlands. The Bena strip took just five days to build; located at a height of 5,250 feet, it was 40 yards wide by 400 yards long. The initial landing was made by Bob Gurney in a Moth on Christmas Day 1932. He had as passenger Jim Taylor.

Mount Elimbari, Chimbu District

Bena strip, tiny, unnoticed — its very site forgotten today — was to be the base for the great work that now followed.

Prospects around the Bena base were promising enough for N.G.G. to ask for a more searching examination. With Charles Marshall, N.G.G. surveyor, the Leahys made a journey from the Bena base in early 1933 and from a spur they saw to the west a huge valley, vaster by far than any they had hitherto seen. It was the valley of the Wahgi, the big river Leahy and Dwyer had found on their 1930 journey. They contacted big, coarse-featured Siane people, who lived in the broken country beneath Mount Elimbari, before turning back to the Bena.

Major Harrison was deeply impressed with Mick Leahy's report and agreed that the great new valley must be prospected and explored. Jim Taylor was just as enthusiastic. He had earlier expressed his belief that the western country could hold a heavy population, and eventually it was agreed that an expedition would be mounted jointly by Taylor and his police, on behalf of the Administration, and by a N.G.G. party consisting of Mick and Dan Leahy and Ken Spinks, surveyor, to explore the Wahgi.

On 6 March Mick Leahy flew in to the Bena with Major Harrison in a Moth piloted by Ian Grabowsky. Jim Leahy, the fourth of the brothers, flew in on the 7th and next day the most important aeroplane flight in the history of inland New Guinea exploration took place.

Grabowsky flew in early that day from Lae in Junkers W34, VH-UNM, heavily loaded with 1,350 pounds of boring equipment — with which to test the Bena flats — food supplies and cans of petrol. The Junkers, powered by a single Bristol Jupiter engine, was fuelled for two and a half hours in the air and the passengers that day were Major Harrison, the Leahy brothers, and the pilot, Ian Grabowsky. The flight lasted for only an hour and 20 minutes, but it confirmed all the hopes of the men who peered down from the lumbering Junkers upon the superb, grassed valley of the Wahgi as it unrolled beneath, heavily populated, chequered with gardens and hazy with the smoke of thousands of fires, all the signs of a truly immense population. A cloud build-up forced Grabowsky to turn back, and when they clambered out of the noisy Junkers all were in a state of intense excitement. 'Not one of the party waited for another to finish the description of what he had seen,' Grabowsky has written. 'Everybody talked . . . of gold, river flats, dredging prospects. . . .' Within days, aeroplanes were flying in the first of the mass of the supplies required for the journey to the west; the final load of supplies was flown in to the Bena on 26 March.

The next day Mick and Dan Leahy, Ken Spinks and Jim Taylor made another aerial survey in a DH50A of Holden's Air Transport, piloted by Tommy O'Dea, thus giving Taylor his first glimpse of what lay ahead.

On 28 March 1933, the big expedition left the Bena for the west, on the most significant single journey ever made in this country. What they found is today history. From the Mai River they walked through the Chimbu and into the Wahgi;

the country they discovered and the people they found fulfilled their most fervent dreams, although they found no second Edie Creek, no Bulolo valley. Fourteen days after the start, Grabowsky landed in a Fox Moth on a hastily cleared strip in the great valley and replenished their supplies and they moved on again, through the teeming thousands of Highlanders, to Mount Hagen, where a base camp was established and an airstrip built. Grabowsky pioneered this airstrip, too, landing there on 27 April in a Fox Moth with the District Officer Salamaua, Ted Taylor, and the geologist Kingsbury as passengers.

Over the next four months they explored to the north, west and south of the Hagen base, finding traces of gold in many streams, but not El Dorado. Two journeys were made to the Wahgi-Sepik divide, and they walked into the Jimi, the Baiyer, the Lai and the Nebilyer. From the summit of Mount Hagen itself they saw, away to the south, the eroded pinnacles of another great mountain: Mount Giluwe, at 13,414 feet the highest mountain in Papua.

Wherever they went, the explorers found new populations, exceeding any previously found. Although they once encountered hostility, there was little bloodshed. But back in the Upper Ramu, where the patrols of the Administration were working to stop the inter-tribal fighting that raged unceasingly, Assistant District Officer Ian Mack was speared and killed, the first white man to fall in the Highlands.

On 19 October the Leahy-Taylor expedition returned in triumph to the Bena base. Over the succeeding years, Taylor and the Leahys made many more expeditions into unknown parts of the Highlands. Space will not permit anything but a brief sketch of these events. The Leahys made five separate journeys from the Hagen base in 1934, climbing Mount Giluwe and penetrating the Wabag country on the most notable of these trips. The Leahys were not the only prospectors to win renown for their exploratory feats. The Ashton brothers — Sid and Lea — and in particular the Fox brothers — Tom and Jack — did very fine work.

As the country was opened, the Administration established a series of base camps and stations at Kainantu, Bena Bena, Asaro, Kundiawa, Goromei, and for a time at Mount Hagen. Patrols commenced the long task of bringing the unruly, virile people under control. The Missions, too, were soon on the scene. The Lutherans were in the Asaro Valley by 1934, and in the Chimbu the same year and then further west at Mount Hagen. The Lutherans purchased their own Junkers F13 aircraft, the 'Papua', to assist their operations. The steady movement to the west of the Lutherans prompted the Catholics, who had already entered the Highlands, to forestall them: the redoubtable Father Ross of the Society of the Divine Word established a station for his Mission at Mingende near Kundiawa and was in Hagen when the Lutherans arrived there. The Seventh Day Adventists were early in the field.

The work of the various Christian Missions in the Highlands was severely restricted following the killing of two S.V.D. missionaries, Father Morschheuser and Brother Eugene, in the Chimbu in December 1934 and January 1935. The prospector, Bernard McGrath, was murdered near Finintegu, in the present Henganofi Sub-District, in February 1934; his body was found by Mick and Dan Leahy. Ted Taylor, District Officer Salamaua, and T. G. Aitcheson, Cadet Patrol Officer from the Kainantu post, were soon on the scene. Their patrol was attacked. 'During the fighting — one of the most desperate affrays recorded in the history of New Guinea,' says the account of the incident in the Annual Report on the Territory for 1933-1934, 'the District Officer and three members of his party were wounded with arrows, and nineteen of the attacking natives were shot dead before the remainder ceased fire and made overtures for peace, which was then ceremoniously concluded on the spot.' A station was then established at Finintegu; patrols into the surrounding country were many times ambushed and attacked before the situation was brought under control. It was from Finintegu, too, that the ill-famed Ludwig Schmidt party had set off a short time previously on their long journey following the route of the Leahy-Taylor expedition of 1933, and then down the Sepik, a journey which resulted in the hanging of Schmidt for the atrocities he perpetrated upon the natives he encountered. The murder of the two missionaries, coming so soon after these events, determined the Administration to declare the Highlands an Uncontrolled Area. Only those missionaries and prospectors of repute who were already established were permitted to remain — under stern movement restrictions — and from this time until after the War, the Highlands became virtually a closed preserve, open to free movement only to the armed patrols of the Administration as they attempted to bring the rule of law to the Highlanders. Some fine officers served in these years — Alan Roberts, George Greathead, Leigh Vial, Bill Kyle, Charles Bates, Ian Downs and others.

Thus far, all exploratory activity has been confined to the Highlands of the Trust Territory of New Guinea. To the south of the territorial border, in Papua, lay another vast Highlands area. In 1935 this unknown territory was penetrated by a famous patrol led by two young officers, Jack Hides, Assistant Resident Magistrate, and Jim O'Malley, Patrol Officer.* This time prospectors did not show the way to the Administration: Hides and O'Malley were government officers, 'outside men' of Sir Hubert Murray's Magisterial Service. All succeeding patrols in the Southern Highlands before the War were led by government officers: Ivan Champion, Claude Champion, Bill Adamson, Allan Timperley, Jack Bramell and Kevin Atkinson. The final major exploration of the New Guinea Highlands, too, was done by government men.

In 1938-39 Jim Taylor and Patrol Officer John Black led the great Hagen-Sepik patrol, a monumental, fifteen-month Administration expedition into the last of the unknown country, west of Mount Hagen right through to the Dutch border. When this journey ended, in April 1939, the broad outline of the geography and population distribution of the Highlands was known. But much detailed work remained for the post-war patrols of the Administration.

* See *The Outside Man* by James Sinclair, Lansdowne, 1969.

In a foggy dawn a hut appears

A man from Gono, Lufa Sub-District. He wears black cassowary plumes and his face sparkles with mica-spotted clay

Below left: Asaro woman with bundle of kunai grass

Below centre: Kamano woman burning off he garden plot in preparation for planting a crop of sweet potato

A young Frigano man addressing his village during a land dispute. The Highlanders are great orators

low right: Pigs, the treasured possessions of Highlands, sleep the afternoon away against the wall of their owner's hut

Above:
A Highlands feast. *(left)* Before the feast. *(centre)* Apportioning the pig.
(right) The head of a roasted pig. Pig is the prime delicacy to the people of the Highlands

Far left: Opening a mu-mu oven and removing the cooked sweet potatoes

Left: Taro, one of the staple foods of the Highlanders. A beautiful lily-like plant, the swollen roots are eaten

2

The People

An earnest lady, overwhelmed by the colour and spectacle of a typical Highlands sing-sing, once said to me: 'Oh, why did we thrust our modern civilization upon these Highlands people? Why did we not leave them alone? They were a simple peasant people; living such uncomplicated lives before we came along!'

Attractive though the thought may be — and many times propounded — it is based upon misconception and superficial observation, and also ignores the realities of history. For violence, pressure and strife are the common denominators of all of the rich and intricate societies of the Highlanders. Their lives are incredibly complicated; they are subjected to a myriad pressures, social, religious and economic: their existence is even more formalized and ritualized than is our own.

It is unwise to generalize about the Highlanders, for although they share many characteristics each Highland society is an entity, with prohibitions and customs of its own. But some general observations might be risked.

The Highlanders are a strongly materialistic people, a people whose culture frequently leads them to violent solutions of their problems; in many of these societies a degree of male-female antagonism is very apparent. Men regard themselves as superior creatures, the carriers of the seed of the race; the women are merely receptacles, to be dominated by the male, and whose fate it is to bear children and to work out their lives in the gardens. Most — but by no means all — of the Highlands clans are patrilineal and patrilocal, recognizing inheritance through the male line exclusively. The Highlanders are farmers, and highly skilled. The staple food is the sweet potato — although a great variety of other foods are eaten — and many varieties are recognized and cultivated, in beautifully fenced and terraced gardens. The most prized possession was, and is, the pig. The people, both men and women, are lovers of ceremony and ritual; they deck themselves with pearl shell, with the gorgeous plumes of the bird of paradise, the feathers of the mountain parrot, the black cockatoo and the cassowary; with the shining shards of beetles and the skins of the marsupials that have managed to survive in this meat-hungry society in the rain-drenched forests of the high mountains.

The lives of the Highlanders are intimately bound up with their land; there is no

Man of Kambasakuyufa, in the Upper Asaro

sweeter sight for the returning Highlander than his land. A great deal of the inter-clan fighting that occurs at times even today — although on a far lesser scale than the mighty battles of yesteryear — springs from disputes over the ownership of land. They are bow and arrow fighters and often carried wooden shields, and axes and clubs of stone. The savage law of pay-back dominates their lives: if one clan injures another, then that injury must be repaid in kind, no matter how long may be the wait for opportunity.

Although the Highland districts are today under full administrative control, after two decades of post-war contact with the patrol officers and their police, the ways of old have by no means been entirely abandoned. It is claimed by some that civilization has sapped the spirit and drained the life-force of many of the peoples of New Guinea. Whatever the truth of this claim in relation to the rest of New Guinea, it is not true of the Highlanders. They have eagerly embraced many aspects of our culture. They love money, and the things it can buy; the motor vehicle is the new status symbol and a surprising number are in the hands of the people. They grow coffee, introduced by the European, as their cash crop. They are shrewd and enthusiastic politicians. Some of them are, like many Australians, over-fond of the introduced beer. But they have retained most of the aspects of their traditional culture that give a meaning to their lives. Only open warfare, cannibalism and certain practices deemed by the Administration to be against the interests of society as a whole are now denied them. Many observers would agree that the Highlanders are making a successful adjustment to the new civilization into which they were so abruptly thrown, just a few years ago.

Let us now look very briefly at the people of the Chimbu, the Western and the Southern Highlands before proceeding to a more detailed description of the Eastern Highlanders, with whom this book is primarily concerned.

THE CHIMBU

Until July 1966, the Chimbu District was an administrative division of the Eastern Highlands, and there is a strong affinity between the border peoples of the two districts. This district has the greatest population density of any of the eighteen districts of the Territory: within the boundaries of the Chimbu live almost 190,000 people, in an area of only two thousand square miles. The district is heavily mountainous; there is very little flat land. The people build their villages on massive, sharp-keeled ridges and make their gardens on slopes so precipitous as to defy belief, for so great is the population of the small Chimbu District that in places the people are forced to utilize the very mountain-sides for their subsistence gardens.

The biggest language group in the Territory is to be found in the Chimbu; the people are fiercely proud of being Chimbu, and when they leave their mountain-locked valleys on visits to the coast they maintain their identity as Chimbu. They

Chuave, Chimbu District

Page 32: Chimbu man. His shoulders are hung with the skins of the cuscus and he wears the breast skin of a bird of paradise across his forehead

Page 33: A Chuave (Chimbu District) woman washing her child in the chill waters of a mountain creek

Far left: Typical village on the Eastern Highlands — Chimbu District border

Left: Cloud choked Highlands country from a Cessna aircraft

Below left: Coffee trees. Shows typical heavy shade cover

Below centre: Mature coffee beans, ready for picking

Below right: Cessna 336 aircraft of Territory Air Lines at Karimui Government Station, Chimbu District

are a physically impressive people, heavily and powerfully built, with a strongly developed love of the material. This has led them to a ready acceptance of many features of Western culture, not the least the Western economic system.

The headquarters of the district is at Kundiawa, a compact and craggily-beautiful settlement on the Highlands Highway, and there are outstations at Karimui — where Leahy and Dwyer passed through, forty years ago — Gembogl, Chuave, Gumine and Kerowagi. The people are mainly dependent upon coffee for a cash income, and most of their crop is purchased and marketed by their own large co-operative society, based at Kundiawa.

THE WESTERN HIGHLANDS

This huge district, containing over 9,600 square miles of mountain and valley, is the most heavily populated of the Territory's districts. Three hundred and twenty thousand people live in the Western Highlands, and so varied and striking are the tribal groups, so spectacular their dress and customs, that their fame has tended to overshadow the other wonderful Highlands cultures.

The headquarters of the district is Mount Hagen, a fast-expanding settlement in the shadow of the great mountain of the same name. There are many sub-district stations and patrol posts: Jimi, Tambul, Minj, Wabag, Wapenamanda, Kompiam, Kandep, Laiagam, Porgera, Kopiago, Baiyer. This proliferation of stations reflects the great number of tribal cultures within this district. For the people are indeed varied: the strange, scattered nomadic Hewa people of the Lagaip — declared under full administrative control as recently as 1971 — the wig-wearers of Lake Kopiago, the Porgera and Wabag; the singular Jimi Valley people; the big, bold, colourful people of the vast Wahgi Valley, the most striking geographical feature of the district. It was in the western part of the Wahgi that the great traditional ceremonial exchange festivals known as *moga* were developed to their highest peaks of spectacle and social significance. The *moga* exchanges have lost much of their importance under the impact of our economical system. Before the coming of the European, the *moga* ceremonies — involving the exchange of sometimes thousands of pigs and pearlshells between individuals, clans and tribes on a basis of mutual obligation — gave a flavour, an excitement to life: a man would gain personal prestige in accordance with the number of pigs and shells that he contributed to the *moga* exchanges. Ceremonial exchanges of this type were common in many parts of the Highlands, but it was the Hagen people who developed the *moga* into a social and political institution of overwhelming significance.

Although the Western Highlanders obtain most of their cash income from coffee, they have another introduced cash crop of considerable importance: tea. The product is of very high quality and commands a premium price on overseas markets. Cattle, too, are becoming increasingly numerous.

Bamboos. Typical Highlands mountain scene — Kundiawa, Chimbu

Above: The Wahgi River winds on its way through the vast Wahgi Valley, Western Highlands District

Left: Minj, Western Highlands District with the vast Wahgi Valley in the background

Right: Old Mendi man, Southern Highlands District

Ialibu man, Southern Highlands

Southern Highlands country

THE SOUTHERN HIGHLANDS

This fascinating district, with a population of almost 200,000 and an area of 6,800 square miles, is the only Highlands district in Papua. I have a particular affection for the Southern Highlands: I spent the years 1955 to 1958 there, establishing the sub-district station of Koroba, in the far north-west corner, in the country of the then, uncontrolled Huri and Duna wigmen. The last of the Highlands districts to be explored, the Southern Highlands remains the least accessible and developed, dependent to a great extent on light aircraft for internal communications, and to this day the province of the Administration officer and the missionary: there are but a handful of Europeans in the Southern Highlands in private enterprise.

The headquarters of the district is Mendi, linked by a motor road that climbs to over 9,000 feet around the northern flanks of Mount Giluwe, Papua's highest mountain, to Mount Hagen. To journey on from Mendi to the other district stations — Nipa, Poroma, Margarima, Ialibu, Pangia, Kagua, Erave, Tari, Komo and Koroba — one flies, or walks, although an internal road network is being constructed. Because of the difficulties of communication, the Southern Highlanders have preserved more of their traditional dress, customs and culture than have the people of the three New Guinea Highlands districts. There are five major language groups in the district, and the people have cultural links with those of the Gulf, the Western Highlands and the Chimbu. Almost half of the population of Papua live in this one district. The most magnificent fresh water lake in all of Papua and New Guinea — the sapphire-blue Lake Kutubu, almost thirteen miles long — is situated in the Southern Highlands.

Like all of the Highlanders, the people of this district were in the very recent past great warriors. They fought with each other, and when the first government patrols entered their country they fought with the patrols. The Huri, in particular, were skilled in war: they fought what amounted to regular campaigns, with opposing armies of bowmen numbering many hundreds and even thousands. They were merciless fighters, razing houses and gardens, destroying banana groves and killing and mutilating the pigs of the enemy.

Because of the isolation of the district, there is as yet limited economic development. An attempt is being made by the Administration to establish tea as a cash crop, and there is no doubt that cattle will eventually flourish in many parts of the district.

From the Southern Highlands, the least developed of the districts of the Highlands, we will now turn to the Eastern Highlands, the most developed.

THE EASTERN HIGHLANDS

The Eastern Highlands District covers an area of some 4,600 square miles of grassed valleys separated by high mountain ranges. The district is bounded by the

Chimbu, Madang, Morobe and Gulf Districts and with a population of around a quarter of a million is one of the most densely populated districts in Papua and New Guinea. The Highlands Highway, New Guinea's longest and most important road, runs through the centre of the district on its way from Lae, on the coast, to Mount Hagen and beyond. Almost one thousand miles of roads, in many places trafficable only by four-wheel-drive vehicles, link the villages of the district. Most were built over the past fifteen years by the people, with digging sticks and shovels, under the supervision of the 'kiaps', the patrol officers and their police detachments. They are known as 'kiap roads' to this day. Because of this road network, less use is made of light aircraft in the Eastern Highlands than in the other Highlands districts. Along these roads the light Japanese trucks of the coffee-buyers incessantly roam, for coffee is the principal product of the district. Over 7,000 tons of high quality *arabica* coffee is grown annually; of this total, some 72 per cent is produced in the coffee groves of the villagers. Cattle raising is becoming important to the Eastern Highlanders. A cash crop of secondary importance is passionfruit; the fruit is processed at an ultra-modern factory at Goroka, the principal town.

Goroka, a beautiful garden settlement at a height of 5,200 feet, has grown from an airstrip and a collection of grass-roofed houses in only twenty years. A town of some six thousand Highlanders and fifteen hundred Europeans, it is the administrative headquarters of the district. In common with the other districts of Papua and New Guinea, the Eastern Highlands is divided into sub-districts, each station staffed with the representatives of the different departments of the Administration: the Assistant District Commissioner, the Rural Development Officer of the Department of Agriculture, the doctors and medical orderlies of the Public Health Department, the Local Court Magistrate of the Department of Law, and others. There are six sub-districts in the Eastern Highlands: Kainantu, Okapa, Henganofi, Lufa, Goroka, and Wonenara, home of the only Highlands representatives of the tribe of fierce little bark-cloaked fighters known until recently as the Kukukuku.

Kainantu

As we have seen, Kainantu was the first government station to be established in the Highlands. It is a well established township today, the houses and business establishments grouped tightly around the airstrip. Nearby is Aiyura, the Highlands Experimental Station of the Department of Agriculture, and Ukurumpa, the headquarters of the Territory-ranging Bible translation organization, the Summer Institute of Linguistics.

The Second World War had virtually no direct effect upon the Eastern Highlands; there was a little Japanese patrol activity near Kainantu, and some strafing of Administration and Mission establishments by Japanese aircraft. With

Kwateri man, in full traditional Kukukuku dress. This is the everyday dress of these people, not ceremonial dress, and their principal weapon is the bow and arrow

Goroka — aerial shot

Asaro woman framed by the leaves of her coffee tree

Native-owned cattle

Waterlily, Goroka

Goroka market scene — on sale are peanuts, corn, sweet potato and lemons

Road building, Obura. Cutting the preliminary track through the heavy timber

Obura people building a motor road. They want the road as the coffee buyers will then come in with their trucks

48

Road building in the Dunantina

Highlands road building, new style.
The Okapa Local Government Council
operates several modern units. The
deep red clay is typical of much of
the Highlands

49

the end of the war came the re-establishment of civil administration, and the completion of the exploration of the big Kainantu Sub-District. Many people to the south and south-west had not been contacted by the pre-war patrols: now, in the late forties and early fifties, Kainantu patrols led by such men as Ian Skinner, Don Grove, Gordon Linsley, Alan Timperley, Gerry Toogood, Harry West and Bill Kelly began to probe the country of the Tairora, the Fore, the Agarabi, the the Suwaira, the Obura, the Lamari and the Aziana. The patrols encountered relatively dense populations of warlike Highlanders, living in stockaded villages and much engaged in internecine strife. Even today, the people of the Kainantu Sub-District are quick to resort to the bow and arrow when their tempers flare.

Like all the Highlanders, they treasure their pigs and greatly indulge them. The women look after young pigs with great tenderness, hand feeding them and sharing with them the sleeping huts. Both men and women are clever gardeners, the men doing the initial heavy clearing and fencing, the women planting the crops and weeding and harvesting them.

One day the open grass of the Arona and the Ramu will carry many cattle. The Arona Valley is the site of the vast Upper Ramu Hydro-electric Scheme, and in 1971 the Territory's House of Assembly resolved by a majority vote to make the Arona the site of the future capital of the Territory.

There is a small patrol post in the Kainantu Sub-District: Obura, in the south. A patrol officer is in charge here, responsible for the administration of a broken, lightly populated corner of the district. The Obura people are anxious to build more roads into their country, to attract the coffee buyers.

Okapa

The Okapa country, south-west of Kainantu, was untouched before the War; officers who did pioneering patrol work in this sub-district twenty years ago include Ian Skinner, Les Williams and John MacArthur. It was from the Fore-speaking territory of the Okapa Sub-District that the anthropologist Dr R. Berndt first reported, in 1951, the terrible disease known as *kuru*, a fatal neurological disease found nowhere else on earth, that mainly strikes down adult females. *Kuru* has been intensively studied by many medical researchers, most notably by Dr Vincent Zigas and Dr Carleton Gajdusek; the latest theory is that the disease is passed on by the consumption of organs from the dead body of a *kuru* sufferer. For the Fore people had a long history of cannibalism; indeed, descriptions of some of their old customs make grim reading. *Kuru* appears to be on the wane.

Other important tribal groups found in this large sub-district include the Kuwepu, the Auyana, the Gimi and the Keiagana-Kanite. They are all typical mountain Highlanders, living in beehive huts, fond of dancing and decoration, making their gardens on steep terraced slopes and growing coffee as their cash

Kainantu, showing the airstrip

Aiyura: the Highlands Agricultural
Experimental Station operated by the
Department of Agriculture, Stock and
Fisheries. In the foreground, the Professor
Schindler Memorial Primary School

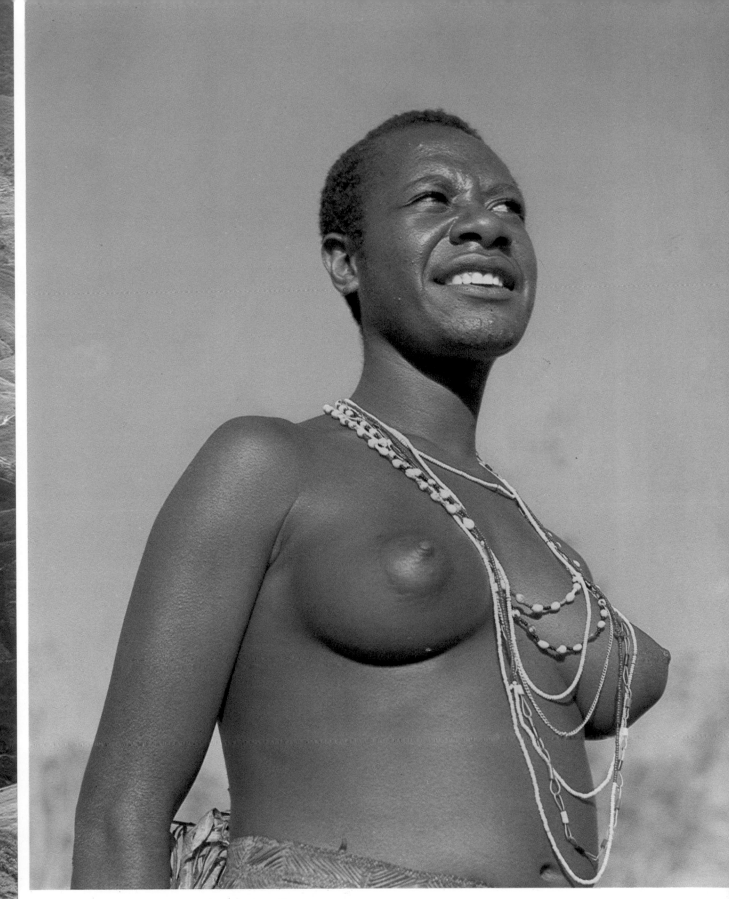

A strapping Kamano woman from Benaga village

A hamlet of Himerata, a mountain village in the Dogara, Obura Patrol
Post administrative area. Fine sweet potato gardens flank the huts of this
family group

A Keiagana mountain village, Okapa

crop. Sweet potato is their staple food, but taro, bananas, pitpit and corn are also important. Animal flesh is greatly prized; anything living that is remotely edible is consumed, but pig is the ultimate food. The country is green and heavily wooded; bamboos and wildflowers are everywhere. It rains very often. By Highlands standards much of the Okapa Sub-District is wet country. Okapa station itself is a beautiful place. The houses of the public servants who staff the station are built on flats and ledges on the ridge upon which the station is built.

Henganofi

A trim little station, Henganofi is situated right on the Highlands Highway, halfway between the townships of Kainantu and Goroka. It was opened by Tom Leabetter in 1949. From Henganofi the people of the Kafe, the Faiyantina and Dunantina are administered. Likeable people, the Henganofi are fortunate in their rich river valleys and fertile hill slopes. They are a milder people than those of the Kainantu and Okapa Sub-Districts; the spirit of aggression has perhaps waned in them, but they are Highlanders still and a clan will not lightly suffer a wrong.

The Dunantina is the most beautiful river in the Eastern Highlands. By dint of much effort, the people have built a motor road into the headwaters from the Highlands Highway and now loaded coffee trucks every day follow the steps of Leahy and Dwyer.

Many villages in the Kafe are sited high up the mountain slopes and in wet weather a shroud of mist will cover some villages for days at a time. At dawn in the Faiyantina the blue smoke from village cook fires fills the valleys with a thin haze as the women cook sweet potato and taro for the morning meal.

Lufa

Few stations in all of New Guinea can compare with the situation of Lufa. Built on a small plateau at a height of six and a half thousand feet, beneath the eroded peaks of Mount Michael, Lufa looks across a great broken valley to the folded, colour-hazed mountains of the Unggai; nearby, the Asaro River winds on its way through steep twisting gorges to its junction with the Wahgi and so, eventually, to the Papuan Gulf. The station was established in 1955. A good bush road links Lufa with the Highlands Highway: there is no airstrip, for this country is too broken. Accidents are not uncommon on these bush roads.

The Lufa — the Labogai, the Yagaria and the Unavi — are in many ways the most likeable of the Highlanders. Much of their territory is high and inhospitable; life can be a struggle in such country, but this seems to have bred a spirit of self reliance and assurance into the people. Many of the village leaders are impressive persons indeed: fine featured, intelligent and forceful.

Left: Okapa man with wooden face mask, at a celebration. He wears moss stripped from forest trees high up in the mountains. The Okapa are the only people to make and wear these wooden masks. The mask represents a bush spirit

Right: The same hamlet as in the title page photograph. The character of this magnificent country changes with the change in light. This photograph was taken just before dark

A Kimigomo man from the Keiagana-Kanite Census Division, Okapa. He is looking through his blackpalm bow, strung with bamboo, at the camera

Over: Fore country at dawn

Two young Fore girls. Okapa, Eastern Highlands

An Okapa man, daubed with clay

A man of the Auyana, Okapa Sub-District. He wears ferocious
pig tusks and a headpiece of black cassowary plumes. His face is plastered
with clay and around his neck he wears necklaces of Job's Tears

Kimigomo woman, dressed for dancing. Her headpiece is made from
cassowary plumes

63

Above: Tangkuo village, Kafe Census Division, Henganofi Sub-District.
A typical mountain village

Above left: The Dunantina, late in the afternoon

Left: Hillside gardens of the Dunantina. The people are burning off
another garden area higher up the slopes

The men make much use of the plumes of the cassowary, the feathers of the red mountain parrot and the black cockatoo, in their ceremonial dress. They hunt wild pigs on the slopes of Mount Michael and in the dense rain-forest with fine bows of blackpalm, whipped around with cane lashings for extra strength, the arrow heads of razor-sharp double-edged bamboo. In this harsh country the cus-cus and the tree kangaroo abound and their pelts feature prominently in the dress of the people. Pandanus palms, too, are to be found in their thousands, rustling and rattling in the wind. They produce not only the material used in the walls of many Lufa houses, but also the *marita*, the edible red fruit that is a food passionately desired throughout the Highlands. Wars have been fought over the ownership of pandanus forests. Away up in the moss forest is one of the marvels of the fauna of New Guinea: the bird-of-paradise known as the King of Saxony. Lufa men delight in adorning themselves with the strange scale-like streamers of this most wonderful of birds.

The girls of Lufa are famed for their grace and beauty. Like most Highlands women, child bearing and the constant heavy work of the garden age them quickly, but young girlhood is a happy time for Lufa maidens. They, too, labour, but there are many opportunities to get away from drudgery, and they make light of their work in the gardens and on the village roads that bring the coffee and passionfruit buyers to their land.

The Lufa women are skilled — as are all the Highlands women — in fashioning the net bags which all carry and which are one of the distinguishing characteristics of the Highlanders. The bags are made of fibre which the women work into string, rolling the fibres across their thighs. They carry into the villages the pandanus leaves and kunai grass from which the huts are made. Some have learned to weave colourful blankets on wooden looms provided by the Department of Trade and Industry, using wool imported from Australia.

A love of children is a common enough virtue of most peoples, and the Highlander has a proper affection for his offspring. The Frigano people, in the eastern part of the Lufa Sub-District, particularly delight in the rich adornment of their girl children. These solemn little girls, often so heavily encumbered with the sheer weight and bulk of their shells, plumes, beads and skins that they can barely move, are exhibited by their proud fathers at times of ceremony.

Goroka

The Goroka Sub-District is the largest and most populous in the Eastern Highlands District and includes the colourful tribes of the Bena, the Asaro, the Unggai and Watabung.

These people are the delight of the tourists who flock to Goroka town for the famous Show, held every second year, alternating with Mount Hagen in the Western Highlands. The Goroka and Hagen Shows are world-famed. For a full weekend each year the gorgeously decorated tribesmen pour into the towns in their tens of thousands, a spectacle quite overpowering to those who have never before witnessed it. Favourites among these tribesmen are the Bena people. A proud, robust people, they live in small clan groups in their valley-lands to the east of Goroka and freely wander through the town on market days, dressed in the skins and plumes of the birds and beasts that the hunters snare in the rain-forests flanking the Upper Bena Valley. The girls are often handsomely built and before marriage they go about their affairs heavily decked in shell, fur and beads, little burdened with work. This time of relative freedom is short: men in the Bena and Asaro communities almost completely dominate the female and after marriage — arranged by the male parents — a woman must accept the life of child bearing and garden toil decreed for her by the customs of this society.

The Unggai occupy a high wooded plateau, in small village groups, overlooking the broad valley of the Asaro. These people have a definite consciousness of their group identity. Their plateau, though fertile and beautiful, is isolated and the people have abandoned inter-group warfare. The men make much decorative use of the skins of the small marsupials that live in their mountains; many women paint their faces for the dance with coloured clays, and trap small mountain parrots for their brilliant red and yellow feathers.

In the far west of the district live the Watabung people. Akin to the Chimbu, their features are often bold and heavily marked, and they are solidly built, making much use of animal skins in their ceremonial dress.

But it is in the wide valley of the Asaro that we find the greatest concentration of the Eastern Highlanders. A warlike people of old, they remain proud and self-assertive, very quick to react to any wrong. So densely populated is the Asaro towards its western end that land disputes are inevitable and common. This, too, is a society heavily dominated by the male; traditionally, men in the Asaro lived much of their lives away from their women. Although there are signs that the emerging generation of Asaro women will have more freedom than have their mothers, it is likely that the male will continue to rule the Asaro for a long time to come.

Male initiation ceremonies were commonly found among the Highlanders; many of these have lapsed, but it is apparent that one of their primary purposes was to impress upon the adolescent boys their clear superiority over women. The young Asaro boy was taken from his mother at an early age and plunged into the waters of a mountain stream, thus symbolically washing away the weakening effects of close association with his mother. His tongue and his penis were lightly slashed with a bamboo knife — a further purification; long lengths of cane were thrust down his throat into the pit of his stomach, with inevitable results, and folded lengths of sharp green pitpit leaves harshly rammed into his nostrils and savagely withdrawn to induce copious bleeding. The sacred *nama* flutes of bamboo once brought death to any female who laid eyes upon them.

Lufa station. Shows a typical split-timber garden fence. In the background, the Unggai mountains

A fine Yagaria man

Right: Stalwart young girls from the Yagaria (Lufa) at work with pick and shovel

Below right: Yagaria garden hamlet

A strapping Kamano woman from Benaga village

A Yagaria woman tenderly carrying her pig

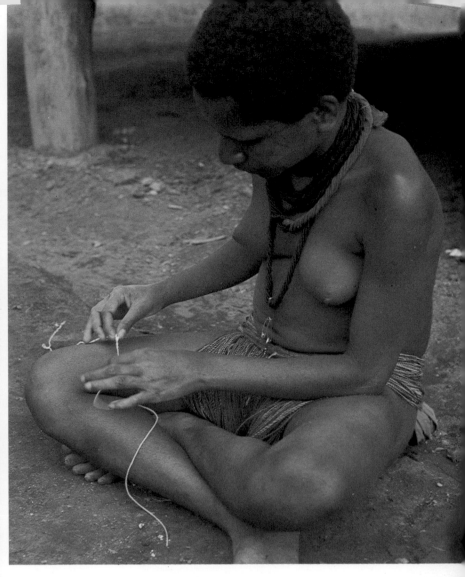

Above: Unavi girl (Lufa) rolling lengths of fibre into string

Above left: Storm clouds break over Lufa station

Far left: Man of the Labogai (Lufa)

Left: Handwoven blankets made at Lufa

A young girl from the Labogai (Lufa) carries home her net bag of food, together with her spade, in pouring rain

Frigano man. The strange King of Saxony bird of paradise plume is particularly fine

Page 76: Frigano man. He wears the perfect plume of the King of Saxony bird of paradis together with a fine marsupial skin

Page 77: Beautiful young girl from Kokalugureinaga, in the Bena Valley

Bena mother with her child

Little girl from the Frigano, Lufa Sub-District, dressed for the dance. Fond parents in the Frigano lavish great care and attention on their children. Across her body is fastened a huge cuscus fur. She has a forehead band of scarab beetles

Page 80: A stalwart man from the Bena. Cuscus fur and the shards of scarab beetles form much of his decoration

Page 81: Bena widow in mourning for her man — she is covered with Job's Tears

These customs belong to the past, but they are a potent reminder of the nature of the Asaro male, brought up from birth to look with superiority upon women and to prize aggressiveness and force as virtues above all others.

It is the male bird-of-paradise that wears the gorgeous plumes for which the species is famous; the male Asaro, too, outshines his women when dressed for the endless rounds of ceremony — for births and deaths, betrothals and marriages, the formal ending of a dispute — that give flavour to his daily existence. Nowhere else in the Eastern Highlands can one find a more brilliant use of colour, of shell, of plumes. It is in the Asaro, too, that one encounters the strange ceremonial of the mudmen, who have become famous even though there are but a handful of them.

Wonenara and Marawaka

Perhaps the most fascinating of the peoples who live within the Eastern Highlands are those of the Wonenara Sub-District. Properly speaking, they are not Highlanders at all. They have virtually nothing in common, physically or culturally, with the Highlanders. They are of the tribes historically known as Kukukuku, who inhabit a great belt of mountain country between the Gulf of Papua and the headwaters streams of the Watut River in the Morobe District of New Guinea. The groups living in the Eastern Highlands, isolated from their parent tribes by the great mass of the Kratke Range, are the extreme representatives of their race: nowhere else in in the Highlands are they to be found.

I have a particular interest in these people, for in 1951 as a patrol officer of the then Department of District Services and Native Affairs I led a seventy-day exploratory patrol from Mumeng in the Morobe District, over the Kratkes, and made the first European contact with these people. When I returned — this time in a little Cessna aircraft — in 1968, I found little outward difference in their dress, appearance and equipment, although it was soon apparent that the cannibalism and the savage inter-group warfare that had been rife seventeen years before were indeed things of the past. With a sense of humility, I learned that these people, with no other yardstick to serve them, used my 1951 visit as their historical datum point, the beginning of their modern time line.

This is rough, broken country. There are but eight thousand of the Wonenara-Marawaka people, but they are scattered over an appreciable proportion of the south-eastern corner of the district. Theirs is the only territory isolated by difficult terrain from the road network that links the villages of the Eastern Highlands. To get in to this rugged country, one flies — or walks.

Flying into the only commercially operational strip in the area — Marawaka — is not for the faint hearted. The airstrip, built by the people under supervision of patrol officers, is small and is currently operational only for light single engined aircraft such as the Cessna 185 and 206 models. Although a perfectly safe airstrip, the pilot cannot afford to make mistakes in his approach, or upon takeoff. Marawaka is the present-day site of the administrative headquarters of the sub-district, which is still called the Wonenara Sub-District, since the first station was established in the Wonenara Valley, to the north. The Wonenara strip was so marginal that in 1968 the Administration decided that a new airstrip and station must be constructed at Marawaka. The move involved the carrying of many supplies and much equipment over the 9,000 foot mountain separating the two valleys, but Marawaka today is well established. The Lutheran Mission has commenced the construction of a station at the opposite end of the airstrip to the Administration station.

Although the Marawaka people are so completely isolated from their parent tribes, they retain the dress and culture that characterize these people. Men and women, small-statured, wear the *malo*, a cloak made from the pounded bark of the mulberry tree, suspended by a bush fibre string from the head. The men wear thick layers of grass skirts around the waist, and across the shoulders, plaited bands of black and yellow, woven from the thin pliable stems of ground vines. The nasal septum is invariably pierced — this takes place during the initiation ceremonies of the young boys — and usually carries a pig tusk, or a quill from a cassowary plume, often decorated with lashings of yellow cane. Men and women are fond of shell decoration, principally the different varieties of cowrie, and the gleaming mother-of-pearl.

The bow and arrow is the principal weapon; bone knives, made from the leg bone of the cassowary, and clubs of stone and wood were commonly carried. When I first saw these people, they were renowned as the 'saltmakers', manufacturers of a coarse and bitter 'salt' from the distilled ashes of the pitpit, a relative of the sugarcane family which is common throughout New Guinea and which provides the shafts for the typical New Guinea arrow. But salt manufacture is a thing of the past, killed by the greatly superior product of the white man.

These people were once cannibals, savage fighters with an awesome reputation and, sensibly, feared by their neighbours. Today, they have abandoned these anti-social habits almost entirely and spend their days in subsistence gardening, tilling the rich pockets of soil around their villages of round grass-thatched huts.

Left: An old woman of the Bena. There is character in every line of her face

Right: Typical 'business truck' collecting kunai grass for roof thatching, near Goroka

Below right: At the top of Daulo Pass, 8,175 feet above sea level. The Highlands Highway crosses this pass on its way through to the Chimbu District

Below: Unggai women swaying and singing in a dance

A beautiful little girl of the Frigano, Lufa. Mountain parrots have provided her headdress and across her chest she wears the heavy skin of a marsupial possum. On her forehead she wears her father's Luluai badge. With the coming of Local Government, the offices of Luluai and Tultul (government-appointed headmen) have lapsed

Above right: Unggai woman looks boldly into the lens

Children at play in the Bena River

Left: Asaro people celebrate the opening of the Minogere Hostel, a business enterprise of the Goroka Local Government Council

Nodofonoyufa woman, Asaro Valley. She is strikingly dressed for dancing

Lunipe mother with her sturdy child

Asaro men preparing pitpit for weaving into sheets to form the walls of a new house. The pitpit stalks are pounded with a wooden mallet prior to weaving

Bundles of kunai grass are lashed to sapling rafters with bush rope to form a thick, weather-proof roof

Weaving the pitpit wall matting

The house is well under construction

Unggai man

Asaro woman working in her peanut garden

Asaro man. His necklaces are made from dog teeth

An old man using stinging-nettle leaves as sandpaper to smooth down his axe handle

Blue Mountain butterfly, Goroka

Below right:
Asaro girl, from Gameyufa near Goroka

Kama leader. These people have a deep love of colourful decoration. They were renowned fighting men

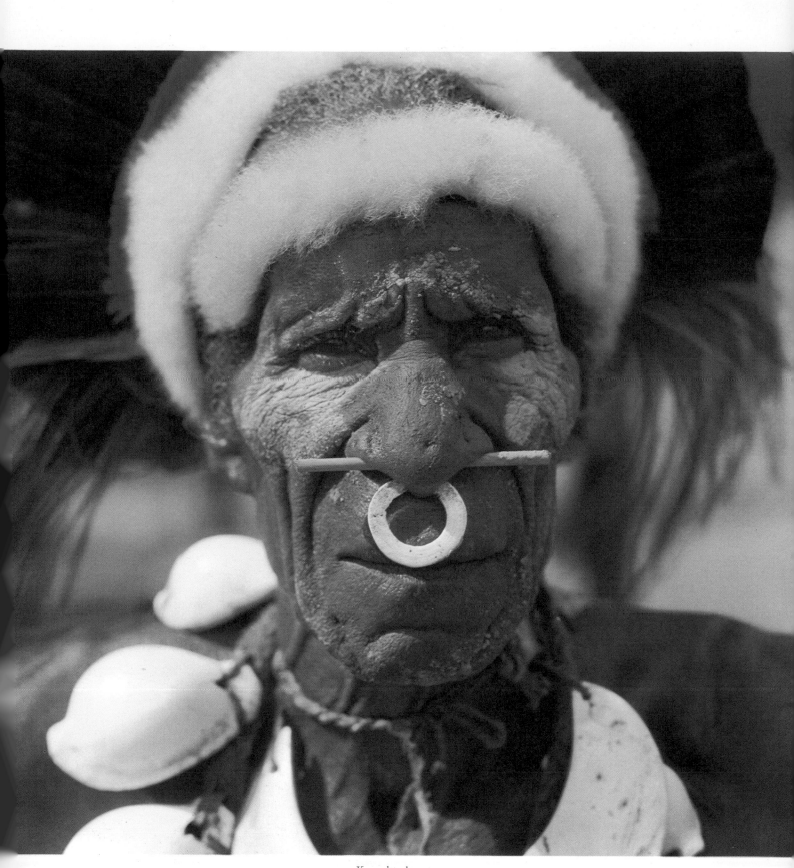

Kama headman

Kama. Note the detail on the arrowheads

An Asaro belle. Asaro girls are fond of this type of decoration

Young Marawaka man makes fire by traditional methods — with a strip of bamboo, a piece of dry wood and tree bark

The Lamari wends its way through rocky gorges

Above right: A Dogolau man, working on the new Marawaka airstrip

The Marawaka people building the airstrip. The strip is vital to Marawaka, as there are no roads into this isolated corner of the Eastern Highlands

Young man from Kumbulatnamo village, Yelia Census Division, Marawaka. He has the typical cassowary-quill through the nasal septum, *tambu* shell and woven vine headbands with a small piece of precious mother of pearl in the centre of the forehead. He is wearing the *malo* cloak, and across his chest and shoulders bands of *girigiri* shell, vine beads and large dogs' teeth

Cessna of T.A.L. taking off from the old Wonenara strip, now abandoned

Gateway to the Highlands: Kassam Pass

3

The Road Ahead

I have said before that the Highlanders will have a powerful influence on the future development of Papua and New Guinea. Each passing year confirms this obvious truth.

We have seen how recently it was that the Highlands emerged from their centuries of isolation; because of pre-war restrictions on European entry to these high grassed valleys — restrictions effectively removed in 1952 — it is evident that the modern economic history of these districts covers a period of but twenty years and less. And yet in this brief blink of time the Highlanders have generally accepted the rule of law; they are embracing to an increasing extent Christianity, European concepts of economic development, and the fascinating game of politics. They appreciate the value of education, and what it can do for their children: there is much still to be done in the field of education in the Highlands, and our Members of the House of Assembly never cease their demands for more schools for the Highlands. The Highlanders are on the move.

It can fairly be claimed that the Highlanders owe much to the dedication, drive and devotion of many individual Europeans — Mission, private enterprise and Administration — for what has been achieved, and in particular to certain District Commissioners whose names are household words in the Highlands today. But this is the year 1971. Soon the people of Papua and New Guinea will have self government, and then independence. The people will be then responsible for the destiny of their country. Already they are beginning to produce the leaders of the future.

We thank the system of local government, with all its admitted deficiencies, for much of the progress that has been made. Most of the politicians of the Highlands districts who represent their people in the Territory's House of Assembly were once Local Government Councillors. In the Eastern Highlands, Council administration covers over 220,000 people; only in the isolated Wonenara Sub-District are the people still administered under the old village official system, and soon the new method will be in operation here, too. The Councils cover a wide field of activity. They are financed by head-tax, set and collected by the Councils, and by Administration special-purposes grants. They build roads — increasingly, with modern heavy equipment — bridges, aidposts, schools. The Goroka Council is probably the most advanced in the Territory. The Town of Goroka was the first in the Territory to be included in a Council. Today the Council's budget exceeds three-quarters of a million dollars. It is responsible for a considerable range of community services — road and town maintenance, road and bridge construction, water reticulation, sanitation and garbage collection and disposal, hostel and low-cost housing development, the operation of a fine and widely patronized food market.

Freely elected by his constituents, from a common roll, the Local Government Councillor learns his first basic lessons in democracy from attending his Council meetings and the committee and budget sessions. In most of the Councils there are European councillors, also freely elected. There is in fact throughout most of the Highlands a spirit of trust and mutual tolerance between the Highlanders and the Europeans who have settled among them. There are many examples of co-operation between the different racial elements. The Highlands Farmers and Settlers Association has had Highlanders as members for many years, and many individual Europeans have sponsored and assisted Highlanders in business enterprise. There is an emerging class of exceedingly shrewd and prosperous Highlander businessmen, small at present but bound to become increasingly significant.

Independence will be difficult for Papua and New Guinea if there are not sufficient educated and trained people, and in Goroka is established the Teachers College, one of the key educational institutions in the Territory. For from this college come the secondary school teachers for the Territory's high schools. There are three high schools in the Eastern Highlands, one, at Goroka, operated by the Department of Education, and the others at Asaroka and Kabiufa, run by the Lutheran and Seventh Day Adventist Missions, two of the pioneering Missions who with the other Christian Missions have done so much in the religious, education and health fields throughout the Highlands.

And so the Highlanders advance towards their future. There are problems aplenty ahead; the road will not be 'straight', as the people say, it will be a convoluted road, a difficult road, but the Highlanders will traverse it and come through in the end to their destiny. For they are a strong-minded people.

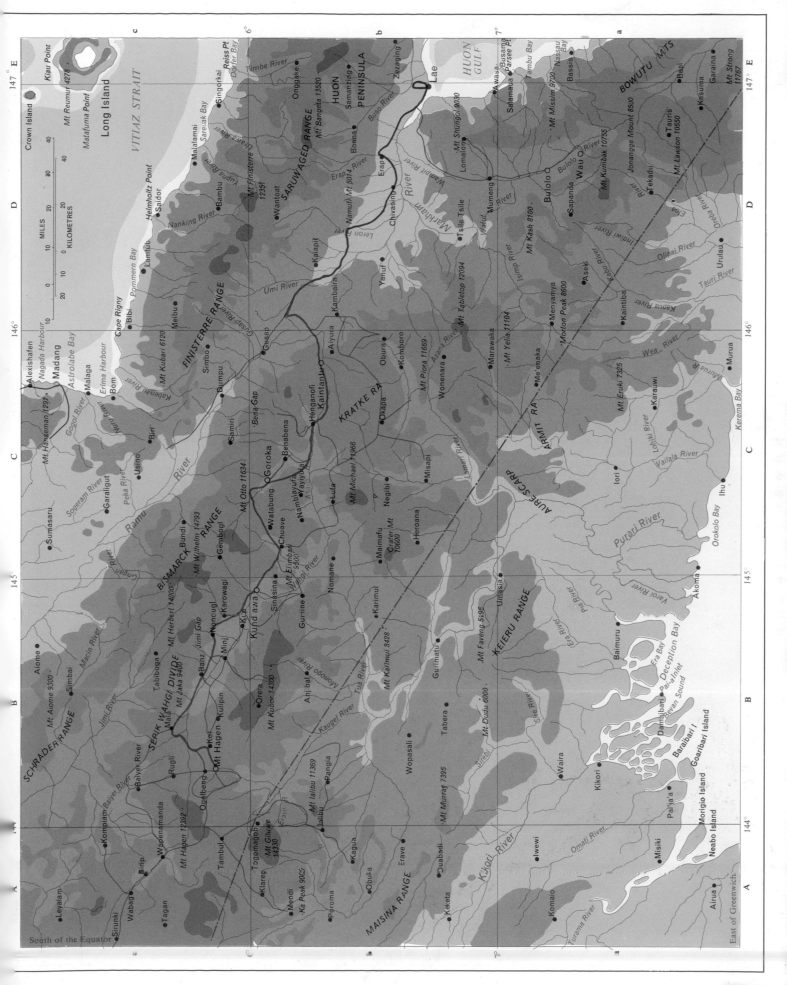

Marawaka Station under construction. The beehive huts are characteristic of the Highlands

Young widow from Kwinandari village, Marawaka, in mourning. Her face is covered with yellow clay; she wears a pig tusk through her nasal septum and she wears the *malo* cloak. Two large *komakoma* shells are around her neck; the smaller white shells are *girigiri*, a small white cowrie used throughout the Highlands as money in the old days

Page 110: A worn woman from the Kwateri settlements

Page 111: Proud young Kwateri man. He wears a fine pig tusk through his nasal septum; also, a particularly good mother-of-pearl crescent. He wears strings of *girigiri* shell and the characteristic Kukukuku strings of braided yellow vine

Dogolau girls

Typical of the bush roads of the Highlands

A little girl from Kwateri village, looking through the split timber fence that
protects her father's garden

A Gaima man, from the Wugamwa, Wonenara. He wears a crescent of mother-
of-pearl and strings of plaited vine skin and *girigiri* shell

Above: Tobacco at Rothmans plantation in the Asaro: a new industry for the Highlands. W. D. & H. O. Wills have a small experimental plantation in the Asaro also, some miles from the Rothmans plantation

Above left. Children at Iufi-Iufa Primary T School at play

Far left: Ansett DC3 aircraft at Goroka

Left: Asaro politicians: Mr Sabumei Kofikai, M.H.A. Goroka Open Electorate *(left)*, and Mr Sinake Giregire, M.H.A. Daulo Open Electorate and Ministerial Member for Posts and Telegraphs

ient receives treatment at the Goroka Hospital

Pottery. The ancient art is studied at the Goroka
Teachers College, where these specimens
were photographed

ents at work in the Library, Goroka Teachers College

Lilies, Goroka. Anything grows in the Highlands

Over: Mount Michael, seen through casuarina tree
grove — casuarinas are found throughout the
length and breadth of the Highlands

Notes on photographic equipment

For those interested in the technical aspects of photography the following brief notes are given. For the record, all of the photographs were taken with privately-owned equipment. No photographic or other business firms have in any way sponsored or assisted the production of this book.

Film: All of the pictures were made on Kodak EX120 roll film. This is the Ektachrome-X emulsion, daylight type, and was exposed at the recommended ASA rating of 64. All film was processed to this rating by Group Color Laboratories, Sydney.

Equipment: Mamiya C33 and C330 Professional twin-lens reflex, 2¼″ square cameras were used, with the following lens/shutter assemblies:

    f4.5, 55mm Mamiya/Sekor.
    f2.8, 80mm Mamiya/Sekor.
    f3.5, 105mm Mamiya/Sekor.
    f4.5, 180mm Super Mamiya/Sekor.

These focal lengths approximately cover the equivalent of 31mm to 99mm in 35mm photography.

The most generally useful lens in my experience is the f3.5, 105mm. Although a simple four element design, this lens is extremely sharp and contrasty. The colour balance of all the Mamiya/Sekor lenses is excellent.

The Mamiya Professional is a rugged, versatile camera with a long bellows expansion and parallax indicator built-in, allowing close-up photography without accessories. There are a great many accessories available, all made by Mamiya, and probably the most useful of these are: CdS Porrofinder, giving eye-level viewing with the convenience of an exposure meter built-in; the Grip Holder and Pistol Grip; the Paramender tripod attachment, for complete abolition of parallax error in close-up focusing, and a series of very useful interchangeable viewing screens for special purposes. Filters, lens hoods etc. are of course available in considerable variety.

The camera stands up well to rough usage, although it is fairly large and heavy. It has two unique distinctions: it is the only twin-lens reflex manufactured with interchangeable lens capability, and it is the cheapest interchangeable-lens 2¼″ square camera available. Prices of lenses and accessories are also relatively cheap, for this type of equipment.

No artificial light sources of any kind were employed.

Labogai woman carrying her child, and a bundle of kunai grass

Marawaka children, framed in bamboo, with the airstrip and station in the background

A boy sits pensively at the Goroka Market drinking a bottle of 'lolly-water' soft drink